# Out of the Ashes

WATERCOLOURS
OF WINDSOR CASTLE
BY ALEXANDER CRESWELL

Foreword by HRH The Prince of Wales

THE ROYAL COLLECTION

This publication accompanies
an exhibition held at Windsor Castle
in Spring 2000.

First published 2000 by
Royal Collection Enterprises Ltd,
St James's Palace, London SW1A 1JR

http://www.royal.gov.uk



This catalogue has been published with the
support of Hazlitt, Gooden & Fox.



ISBN 1 902163 89 3

British Library Cataloguing in Publication Data
A catalogue record of this book is available from
The British Library

Produced in association with
Book Production Consultants plc, Cambridge

Designed and typeset by Jeffery Design
in Berthold Garamond Antiqua

Photography by Eva Zielinska-Millar

Printed and bound in Great Britain
by The Wolsey Press, Ipswich

Distributed by Thames and Hudson Ltd,
181A High Holborn, London WC1V 7QX

COVER ILLUSTRATION: *The State Dining Room, Windsor Castle* (1998)

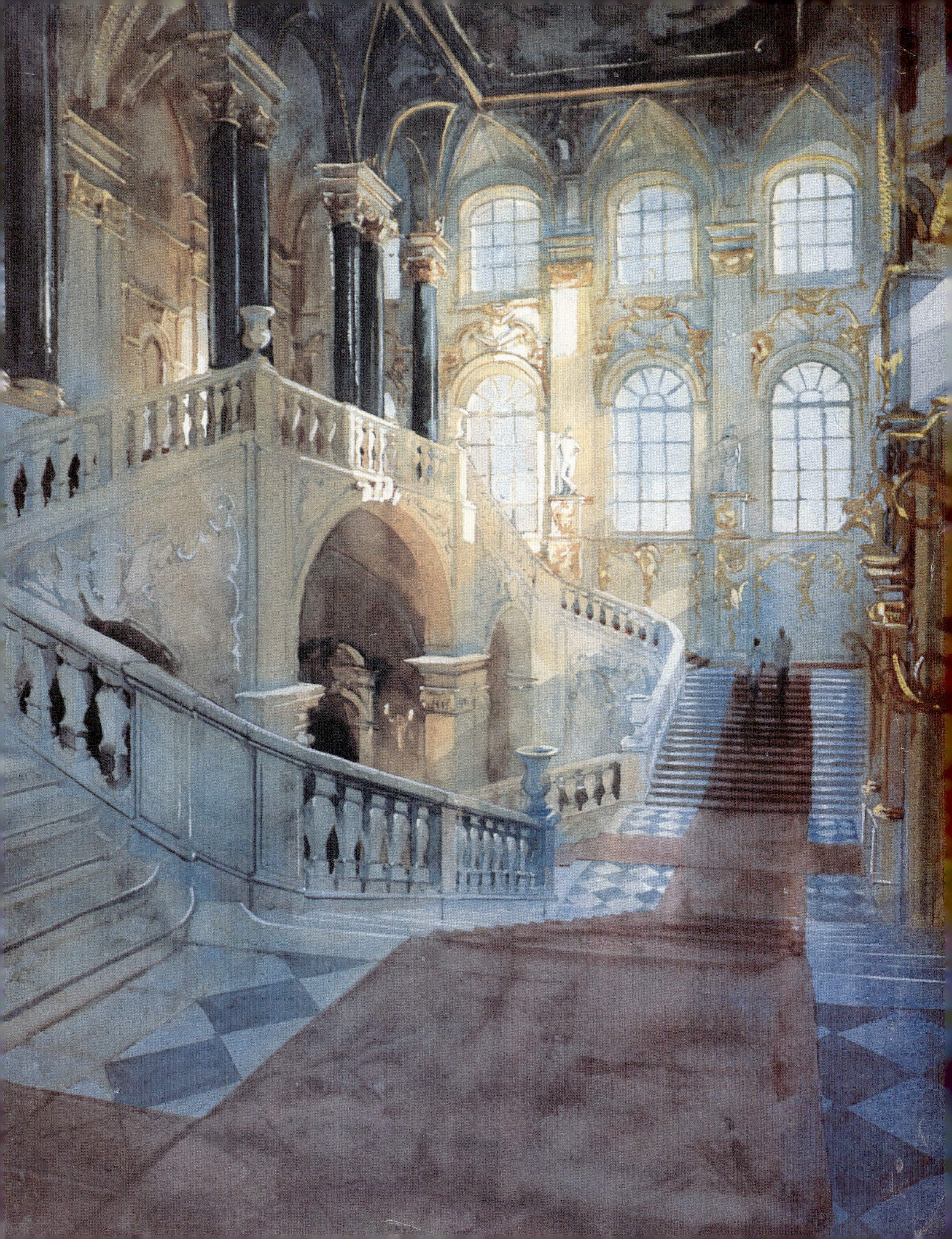

# ALEXANDER CRESWELL

Watercolours

# WINDSOR CASTLE

## AFTER THE FIRE

Eleven watercolours commissioned for the Royal Collection and loaned for this exhibition by gracious permission of Her Majesty the Queen

&

## THE SPLENDOUR OF

# IMPERIAL EUROPE

An exhibition of watercolours from an architectural tour including St. Petersburg, Prague, Bamberg, Paris, Italian villas and English country houses

Wednesday 13 April to Thursday 28 April 1994

Monday to Friday 9am-5.30pm
Tuesday 9am-7.30pm

**SPINK**

5 King Street, St James's, London SW1Y 6QS
Telephone 071-930 7888
Fax 071-930 5710

Overleaf:
The Winter Palace, St. Petersburg
The Jordan Staircase

# Contents

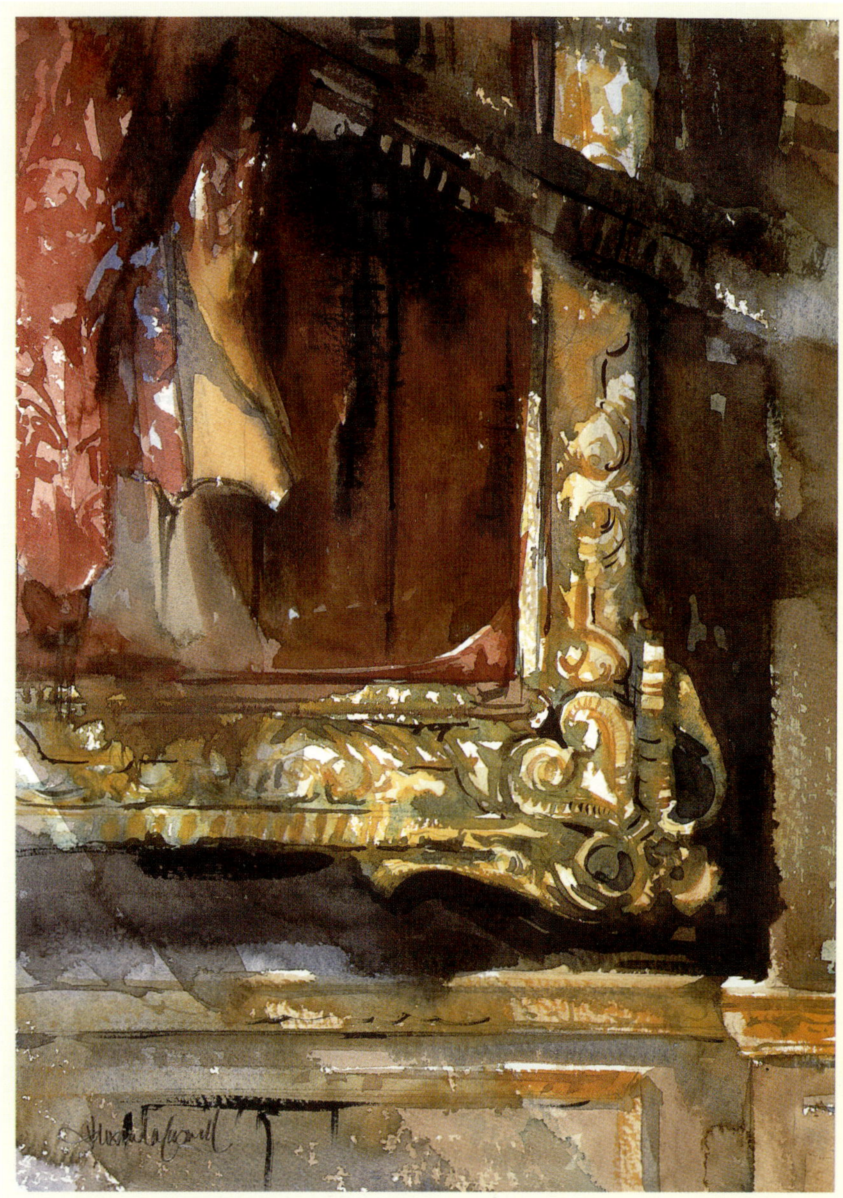

*The Crimson Drawing Room – detail*

King George IV's decoration of the walls of the Crimson Drawing Room in the 1820s included highly ornate frames. Much of the crimson silk within the frames was destroyed in the fire, but some fragments survived. (See also pages 22–3.)

RL 32545
380 × 280 mm/15 × 11 in.
1993

ST. JAMES'S PALACE

The watercolours in this exhibition tell an extraordinary story. Its beginning - the great fire at Windsor in 1992 - was an unimaginable shock, the memory of which needs no prompting. Its conclusion was, in a very different way, equally astonishing, as Alexander Creswell's pictures show; a restoration triumphantly accomplished by the most skilled, dedicated and hard-working team of builders and craftsmen possible.

I greatly admired Alexander Creswell's work before the fire. He has an ability almost unique amongst his generation to capture both the appearance and the atmosphere of a building. I saw this most vividly not long ago when he accompanied me on a tour of Central Europe; night after night I saw places I had visited that day captured with a marvellous immediacy on the pages of his watercolour sketch-book. I felt sure that he was the right person for the Windsor commission - his exhibition immediately before it was of *The Silent Houses of Britain* - and I hope that you will agree that these twenty watercolours confirm the particular suitability of his talent to the task.

Alexander himself describes the genesis of his pictures in his introduction. I would add only that they are a splendid addition to the Royal Collection, which I am sure will be cherished long after the memory of the fire itself has faded - a lasting reminder of a truly phoenix-like renewal and fine works of art in their own right.

Charles

# Introduction

The night Windsor burned was unforgettable. When I was commissioned to paint the aftermath of the fire, I could scarcely imagine the horror that my first visits would reveal.

The damaged area of the castle had been enshrouded in plastic to keep the weather out and the windows were blind, opaque. The inside was damp, pungent and several degrees colder than outdoors. Here and there a gap in the plastic would offer a view of green trees and blue sky in the remote world outside. The damage inside the castle had created a fantasy of a palatial interior suggested by the few details that remained: pats of molten lead formed into strange shapes; rivulets of gold leaf that had dribbled down the walls now shining in tiny pinstripes; fragments of damask clung to their frames, punched outwards as if by some force from behind.

Most of the interior was full of rubble, which was being cleared away slowly. The damp remained; over a million gallons of water had been pumped in to quell the flames, water that had seeped into the masonry leaving a foul mud of charcoal and plaster dust which had begun to rot.

The fire had been savage and yet sly; it had destroyed a large part of the castle and in places it seemed to have stabbed thin tongues of flame through solid stone to lick the plaster and gilt on the other side, as if tasting the next room before devouring it. The water had finally drowned the beast and now a shocking truth remained. This was the heart of Windsor – both of the House of Windsor and of the castle; the seat of monarchy on the one hand and a family home on the other. The Royal Family had grown up here, played here, lived here. Here was I in this private place painting for weeks, gathering sketchbooks full of information and working on this series of watercolours for the Royal Collection.

When I had seen the fire from afar, I had been reminded of J.M.W. Turner's paintings of the burning of the Houses of Parliament in 1834 – great maelstrom images of flames leaping into a night sky blazing orange and red. Those paintings have made a permanent record of an event which is now largely forgotten. The fire at Windsor will be long remembered, but I was conscious that my watercolours would certainly outlast my own memory, and that my interpretation of the place and its spirit would probably endure after the newsprint had faded. I have long been captivated by buildings and their existence within the continuum of time; I have painted the finest stately homes and the most forlorn ruins, but in the great State Rooms at Windsor I approached my task with a mixture of reverence and fear.

As I painted in the early spring of 1993, the plastic sheeting rustled eerily above me in the breeze and pigeons flapped frivolously overhead, brushing showers of dust into my paints. Months passed and it felt less sepulchral as restoration work increased and the atmosphere of hope grew into a bustle of action.

Five years later I was privileged to be back again. The restoration was finished. Interiors that had become as familiar as friends were now restored to splendour. The tragedy was past, fading like a nightmare. I had been invited to paint at Windsor again and to celebrate the restoration with sunlight and colour.

Once again I was daunted by the task ahead of me, this time by the richness and grandeur of the rooms. I redefined my working methods, spending many hours drawing the furniture and objects, celebrating the beauty and gradually getting to know my subject. After the fire there had been little detail in the wreckage, just a strong spirit in the place. When the restoration was complete, the spirit seemed in danger of being drowned by the gorgeous detail. I felt I had to tread a fine line.

Gradually the paintings came together, often after waiting weeks for the anticipated light effect that I was sure would show each room to its best advantage. The spirit revealed itself predominantly as a benign and gentle feeling; while I was painting alone in the rooms, members of staff would pass by – curators, cleaners, clock-winders and wardens – and we would exchange a few words, not in hushed reverential tones under the stern gaze of the portraits, but in a cheerful and friendly way in the sunshine. Windsor was a home again, and yet it was still the revered symbol of monarchy.

The preparation for the State Banquet in St George's Hall was my last and toughest subject – I had been steeling myself for the few hours I would have to capture the greatest spectacle since the restoration. I drew feverishly, and – I am ashamed to admit – rudely ignored the members of the Royal Household who peered over my shoulder.

All too soon the preparations were finished and The Queen had inspected the whole ensemble. The banquet was ready to begin and it was time for me to leave. Out in the December night I realised with a great sadness that the enormous privilege of my task at Windsor Castle was complete. On my way out through the Henry VIII Gate, the policeman on duty remarked, 'Quite an event tonight, sir – quite an event.'

ALEXANDER CRESWELL

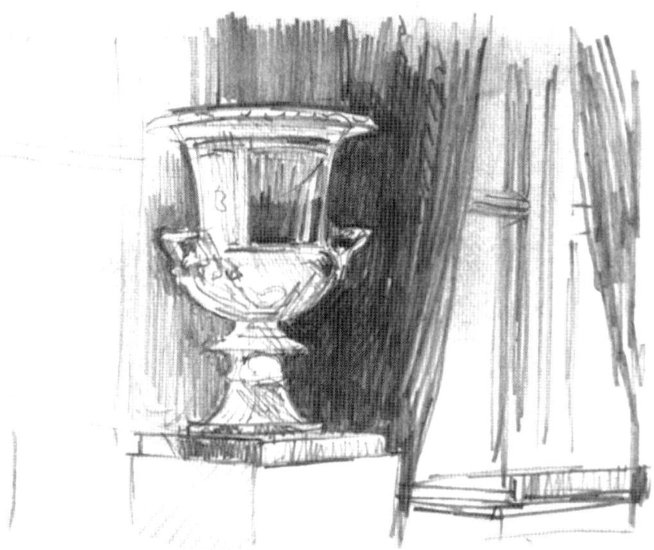

# ST GEORGE'S HALL

When I first saw the interior of the castle, the way into St George's Hall from the Private Chapel was blocked by a plastic sheet, a flimsy replacement for the huge organ that had been totally destroyed. The sheet was then pulled aside to present a view beyond, like the curtain rising on some hideous stage-set; the remains of St George's Hall lay like a gruesome blackened carcass. Roof timbers protruded like broken ribs against the sky. The floor was covered with heaps of rubble and mud. Some of the Garter shields on the walls survived but with their coats of arms burnt off, defaced. Light sconces shrugged in despair, their twin metal lamps melted in the heat. At the far end above the gallery, the plaster relief of St George and the dragon was a barely distinguishable blackened ghost.

St George's Hall was the largest single room to be burnt. I painted it still littered with rubble and debris; a heap of burnt roof timbers is piled up at the far end, while in the centre of the hall stand some of the stone plinths from around the walls. A ladder leans against the wall, having been abandoned after the last suit of armour was hastily removed. The plaster and the panelling are stained a blue-brown colour where water and charcoal have combined into a foul mud that covered the floor and oozed through into the vaults beneath.

OPPOSITE: The original St George's Hall was built by Edward III in the 1360s as a banqueting chamber for the Knights of the Garter, the order of chivalry which he had founded in 1348. George IV lengthened the hall in the late 1820s by adding to it the former Private Chapel at the west end.

Most of the east end of the hall, and the plaster ceiling, grained to look like oak, were destroyed in the fire.

RL 32536
560 × 760 mm/22 × 30 in.
1993

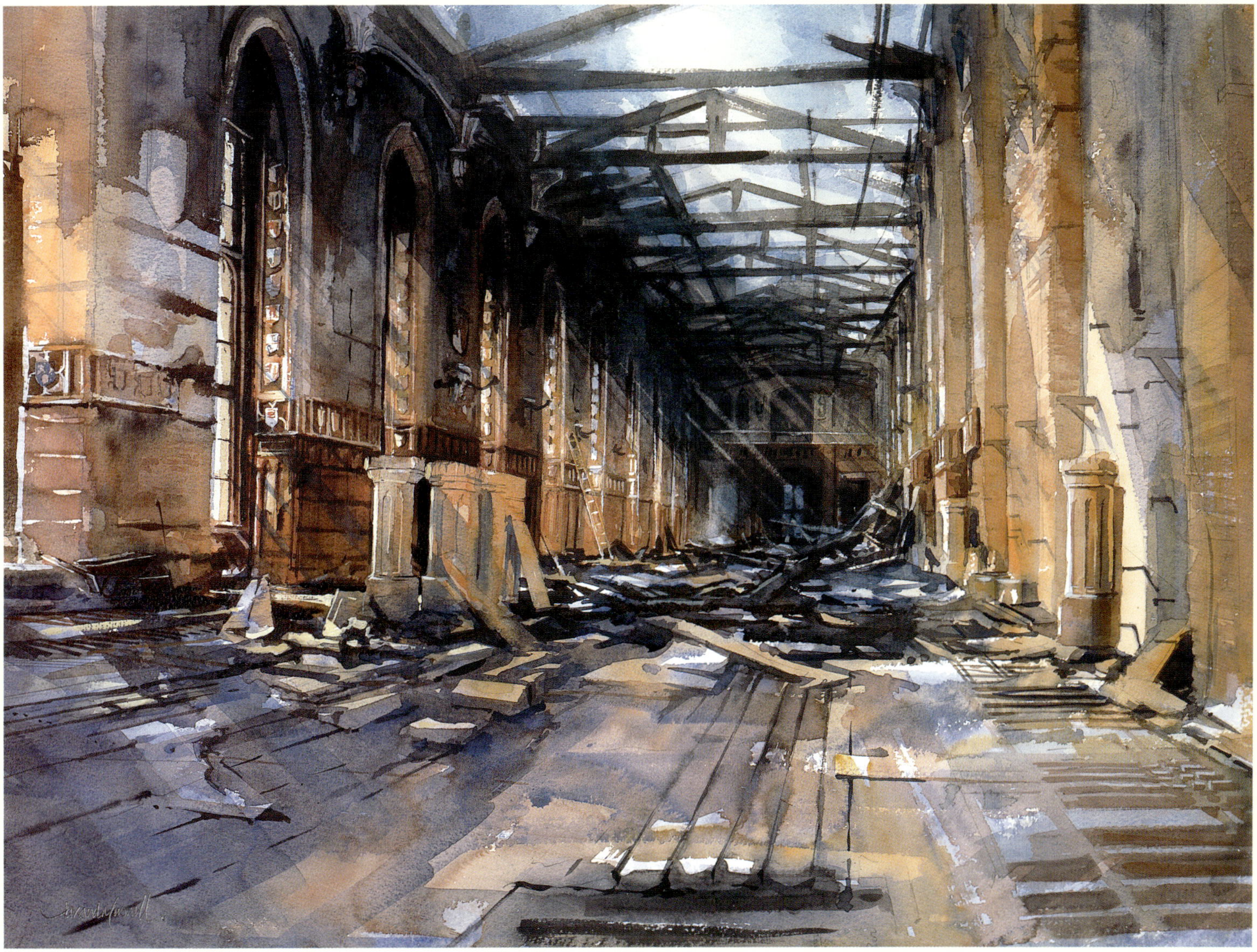

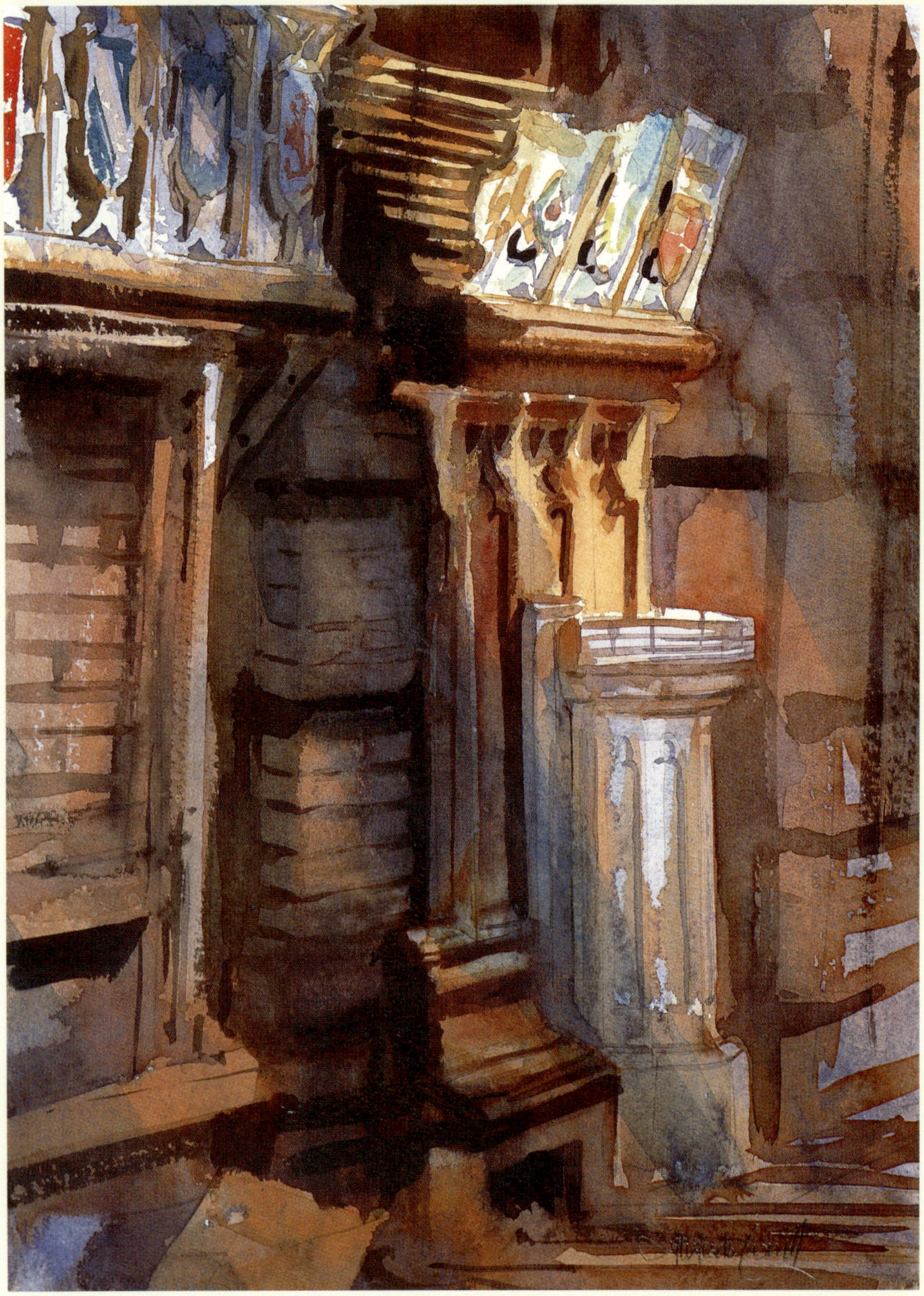


LEFT: Before the fire St George's Hall was decorated with small shields bearing the coats of arms of every Knight of the Garter since the foundation of the order by Edward III in 1348. Because much of the fire was at ceiling level, some of the shields survived, as did most of the plinths supporting marble busts.

RL 32546
380 × 280 mm/15 × 11 in.
1993

OPPOSITE: The gallery at the west end of St George's Hall, and the plaster image of St George and the dragon, survived the fire – as did one small piece of stained glass.

RL 32537
380 × 560 mm/15 × 22 in.
1993

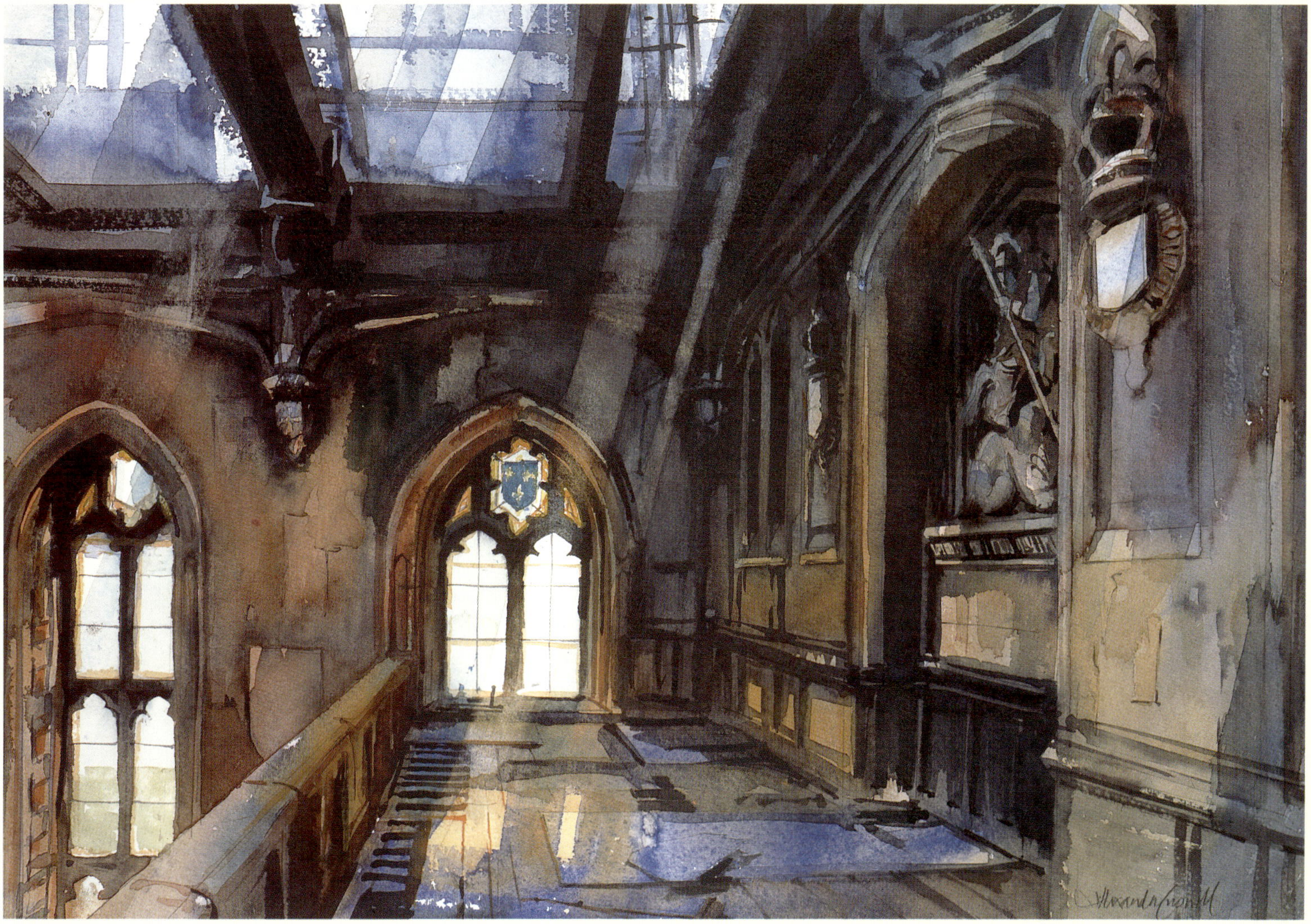

The gallery, just discernible beyond the rubble of St George's Hall (page 9), is a composition in black and blue, relieved only by the clarity of the one surviving pane of stained glass standing out as a beacon of hope amidst the disaster. While I was preparing sketches for this view, the sun pierced the temporary roof above and shone like a spotlight onto the dusty broken floor in front of me. Above, the scorched figure of St George struggling to slay the fiery dragon seemed a hauntingly apposite image in the circumstances.

The apotheosis of the entire rebirth of the castle is the new St George's Hall. I chose to paint it when I was provided with the spectacle which symbolised the reconstruction: namely the great hall laid for the first State Banquet in seven years. This offered me the opportunity to represent the hall at its finest and to continue in the tradition of Joseph Nash, who had painted the same room at the state visit of Emperor Louis Philippe of France in 1844. I had chosen my composition and had drawn the room extensively in the weeks before the banquet; on the night I had a few hasty hours to record the sumptuous table with its receding still life of crystal and gold, the perspective leading away into the haze of hundreds of candles. In the distance a footman is making final adjustments to the table, a hint of the scale of this massive room.

As I drew, each place setting grew as more plate and crystal was carried in and laid with meticulous care at each of the 160 places. No sooner had I drawn one dish than another appeared on top of it, starched napkins covering them up while I rested my pencil. Four glasses at each place soon became seven, and gradually the polished table disappeared under a mosaic of gold and silver, a forest of flowers and candelabra rising above with candle-light filling the whole great space with a warm ethereal glow.

OPPOSITE: The new ceiling, designed by the architect Giles Downes, is the largest oak hammerbeam construction to be built in the twentieth century; it was made in the medieval manner using green (unseasoned) oak. The ceiling and walls are once again decorated with the coats of arms of Knights of the Garter.

The table is set for the State Banquet given by The Queen for the President of Germany on 1 December 1998.

In the new east gallery the King's Champion stands in front of a decorative plaster roundel presented to The Queen and the Duke of Edinburgh by the Commonwealth. The central door in the east wall is open to the Lantern Lobby, where Henry VIII's armour is on display.

RL 33491
560 × 760 mm/22 × 30 in.
1998

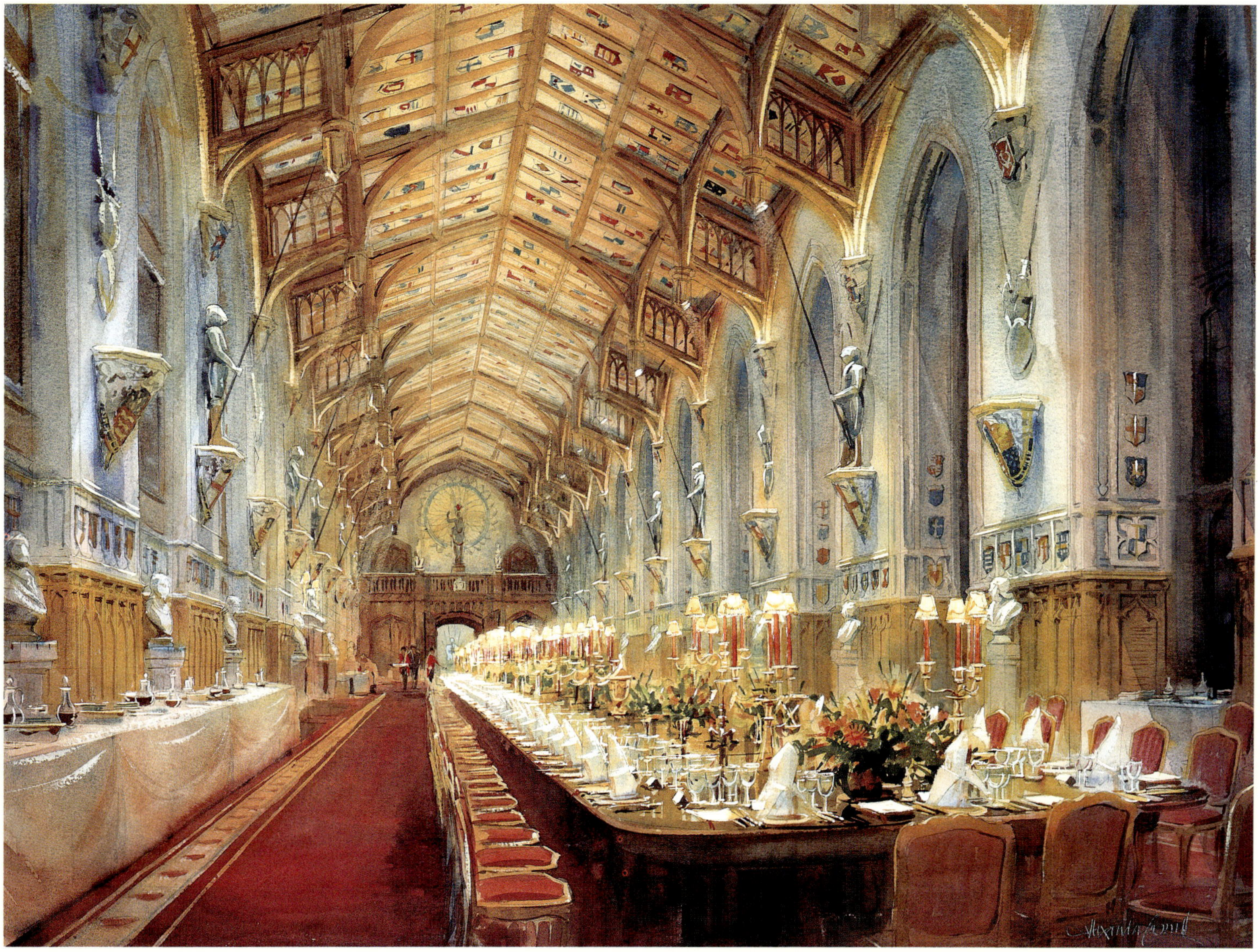

# THE STUART ROOM

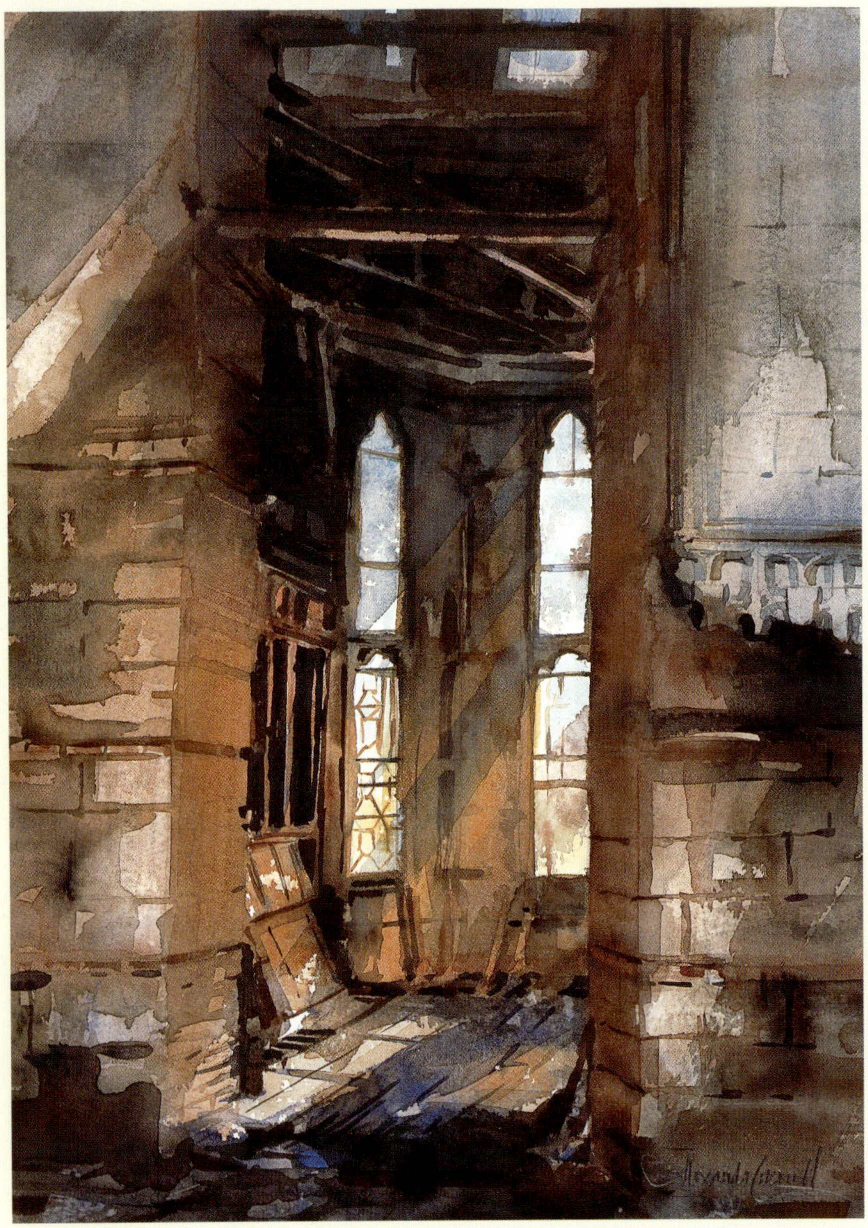

The fire had destroyed both the wall between the Stuart Room and St George's Hall, and that between the hall and the Private Chapel, thus offering me a unique view not seen before or since. A web of supporting beams is visible in the tower above and the twisted and broken windows can be seen through the gap.

In the painting of the Stuart Room after restoration (opposite), these same windows are clearly shown restored, with the charming new staircase swirling up in front of them like a waft of smoke in the sunlight. The brass handrail reflects little sparkles of sun onto the wall, and at the right time of day the new stained glass is projected onto the carpet, making gentle patterns at the foot of the stairs.

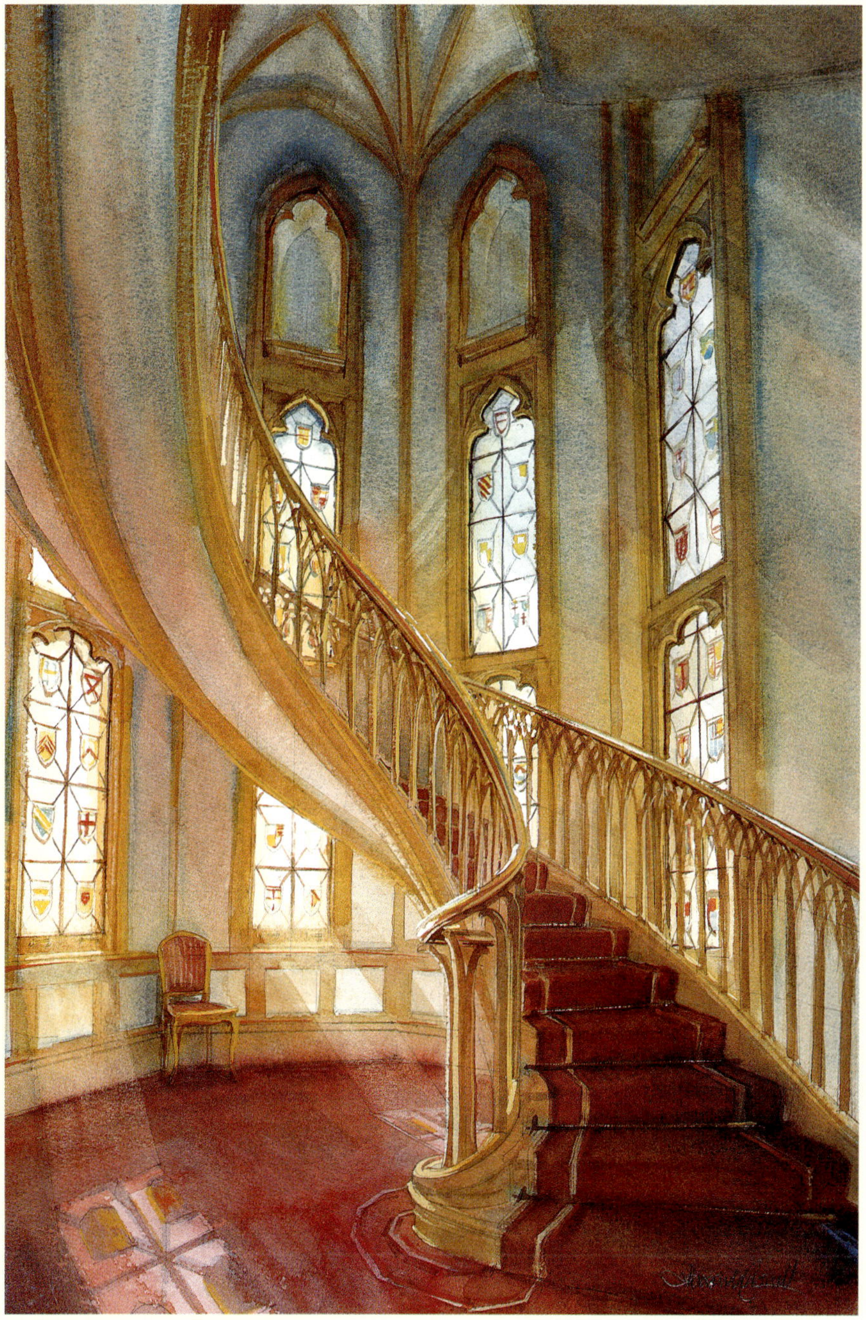

RIGHT: An entirely new elliptical staircase, designed by Giles Downes, now fills the Stuart Room. It rises to the gallery at the east end of St George's Hall. The pierced oak balusters and newel post carved in the form of five rush leaves continue the Gothic theme of the adjacent Lantern Lobby (see page 17). The new armorial stained glass commemorates members of the Stuart dynasty.

RL 33498
560 × 380 mm/22 × 15 in.
1998

OPPOSITE: In the 1920s Queen Mary placed her collection of Stuart memorabilia in this small room. After the collection was moved to the Palace of Holyroodhouse the cases were used to display Renaissance and later gems and other works of art. The cases were destroyed in the fire but the contents had already been removed during electrical rewiring work.

RL 32542
380 × 280 mm/15 × 11 in.
1993

# THE OLD PRIVATE CHAPEL

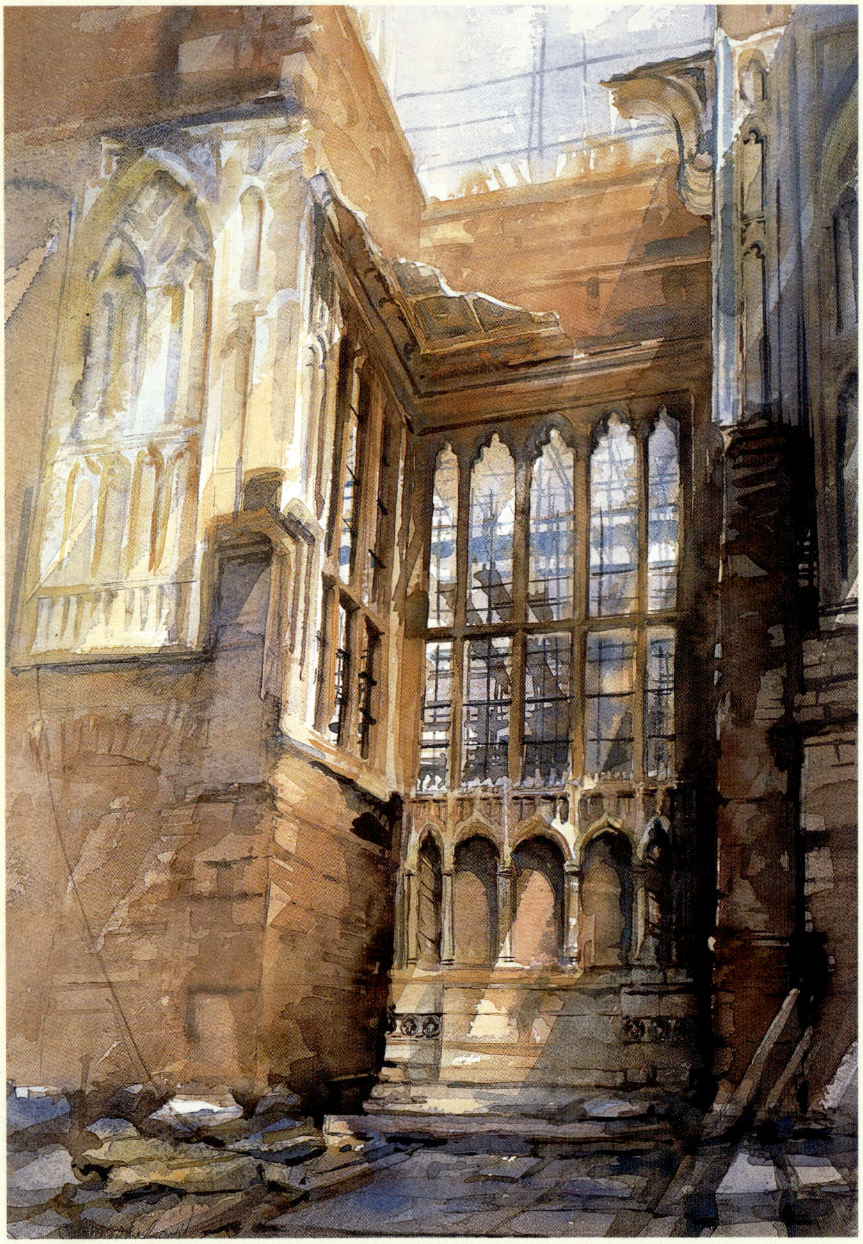

After the fire the Private Chapel was a sickening spectacle, a cavernous space open to the sky. The shattered altar was surrounded by a heap of blackened masonry and charred wood while above it stood the remains of a stained-glass window, its empty tracery pierced at random by baulks of timber. This painting is a contemplation of the remains of the reredos and the window above. The exposure of this room, the Sovereign's private place of worship, to the sky is sacrilegious, the sun's rays intrusive and strident. I have distorted the perspective to emphasise the fragility of the surviving masonry, and shown a jangle of scaffolding that props up the window behind in an attempt to save it for the future.

The Private Chapel was created for Queen Victoria by the architect Edward Blore in 1842, within the space previously used by George IV's private band.

It was here that the fire started on 20 November 1992. The altar alcove (in the centre of the painting) was closed off with two very large curtains. It seems likely that spotlights behind these curtains were the cause of the fire. Although the alarm was raised almost immediately, the fire spread rapidly into adjacent rooms and roof spaces.

RL 32541
560 × 380 mm/22 × 15 in.
1993

# THE LANTERN LOBBY

The Lantern Lobby is the successor to the old Private Chapel, but its new window contains no element of the old. Surprisingly, perhaps, these two paintings are seen from exactly the same point, with only part of the reredos common to both – itself now a memorial to the restoration and a marker of the point where fire germinated from a light bulb. I drew as the summer sun pierced the lantern and danced a pinpoint pirouette on the marble floor; and by autumn, as I had hoped, the declining sun shone onto the reredos itself, reflecting a bright light under the arches with shafts of sunlight standing out against the deep blue of the new vault overhead.

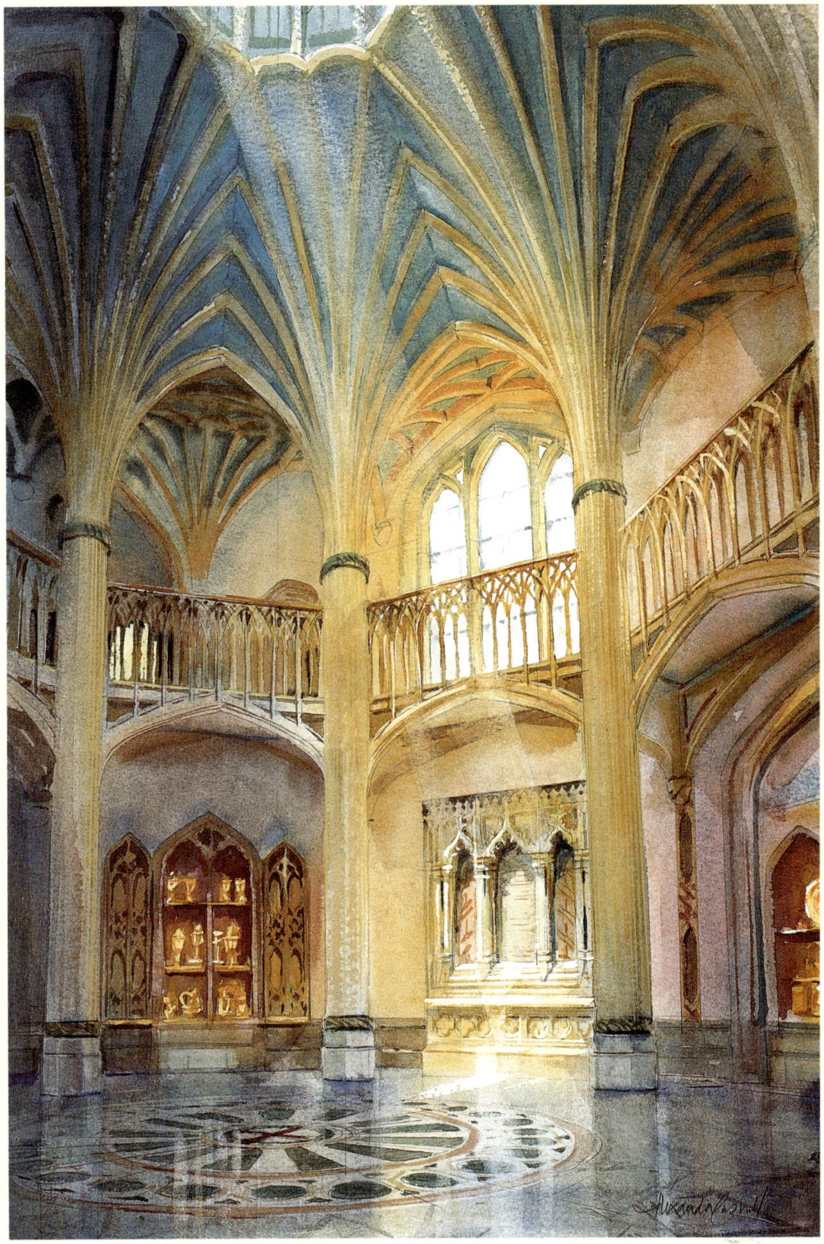

The Lantern Lobby occupies the site of the Private Chapel, where the fire started. Part of the carved stone reredos above the original altar survived the fire and has been retained. The modern Gothic design by Giles Downes comprises eight oak columns supporting a ribbed vault and central glazed lantern. The finely inlaid floor of English marbles depicts the Badge of the Order of the Garter. The lobby provides a new processional route from the Private Apartments to the State Apartments. Wall cases display part of George IV's immense collection of silver gilt.

RL 33496
560 × 380 mm/22 × 15 in.
1998

# THE HOLBEIN ROOM

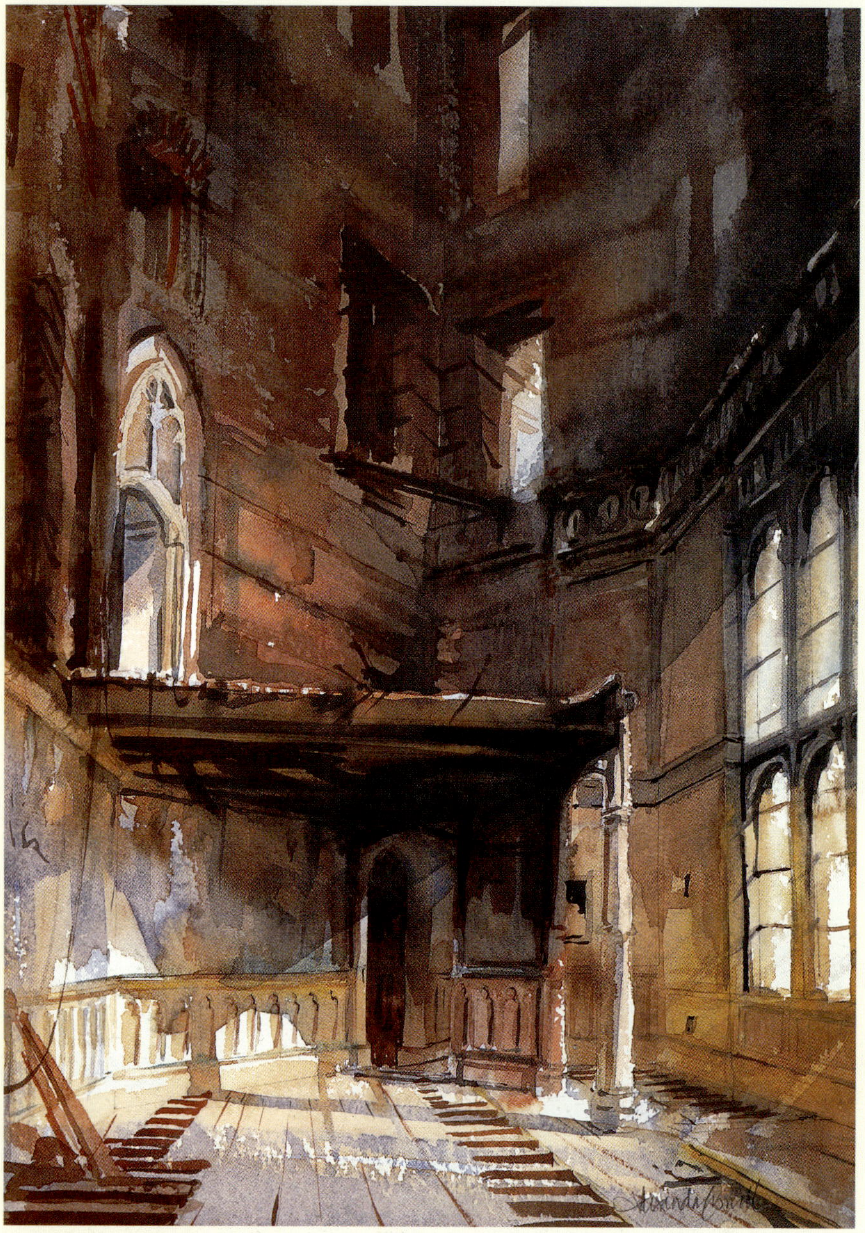

LEFT: Altered by George IV in the 1820s and again by Queen Victoria in the 1850s, this room contained a number of early portraits of kings and queens, and a selection of portrait miniatures – including several by Hans Holbein the Younger (1497/8–1543). Immediately above was the Royal Pew overlooking the adjacent Private Chapel, which was constructed by Edward Blore for Queen Victoria in 1842. The windows on the right now light the new Private Chapel.

RL 32543
380 × 280 mm/15 × 11 in.
1993

OPPOSITE: The new chapel, designed by Giles Downes, incorporates the Holbein Room, which was adjacent to the old Private Chapel (see below). The stained-glass window by Joseph Nuttgens is based on a sketch by the Duke of Edinburgh. The Gothic chairs were originally made for the State Dining Room in the late 1820s.

RL 33497
560 × 380 mm/22 × 15 in.
1998

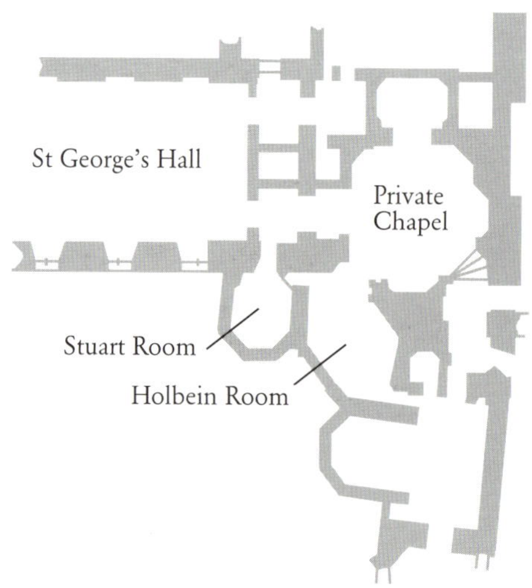


*The location of the Private Chapel before the fire.*

# THE NEW PRIVATE CHAPEL

The new Private Chapel shares its architectural origins with the Lantern Lobby next door, and is roofed with a delicious cerulean blue and golden oak ribbed vault, here looking pleasantly similar to an upturned boat. The new stained-glass window lights up the room like a kaleidoscope when the afternoon sun shines through, and a painting on the right-hand wall allowed me to include another dimension to the light effect. The Pugin chairs act as a measure to show the intimate scale of this room.

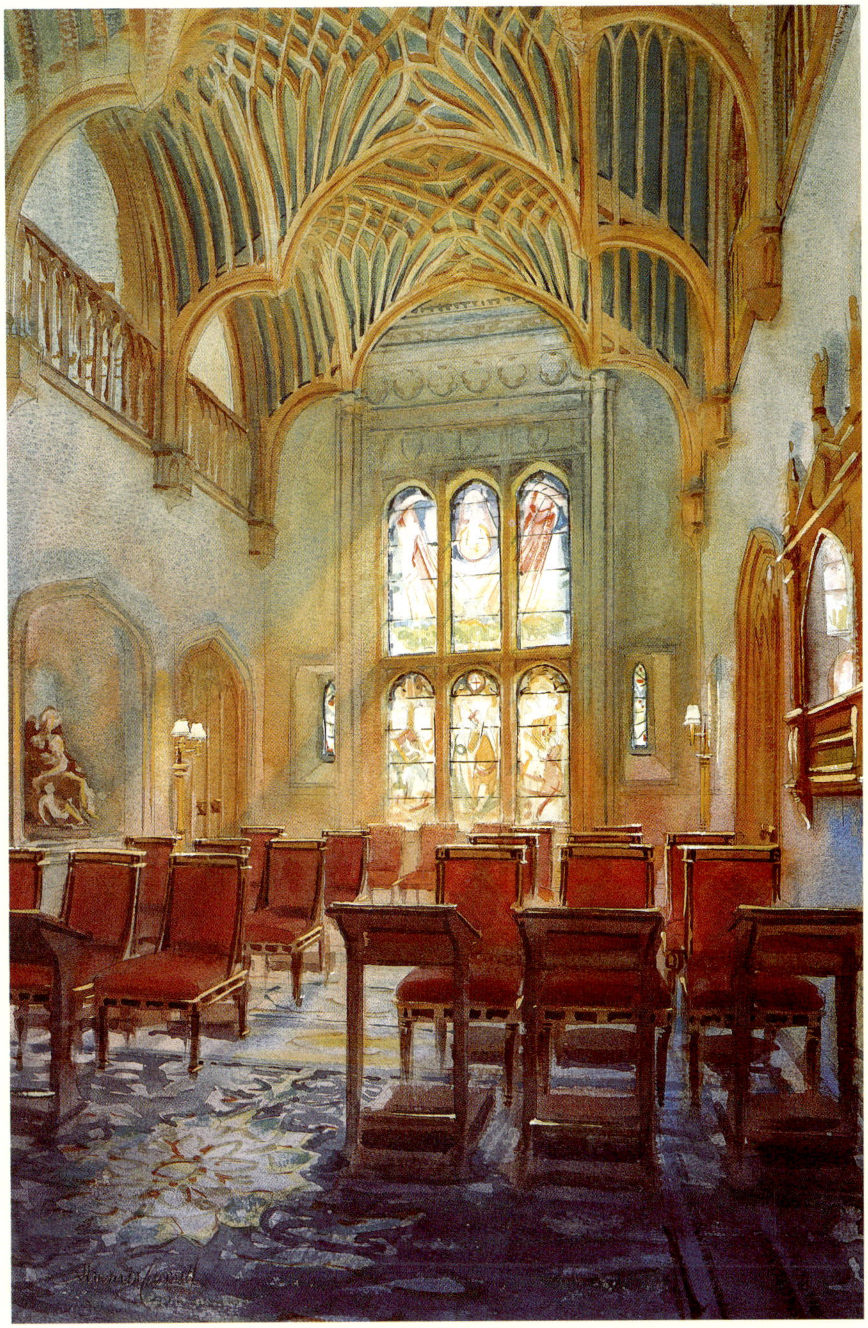

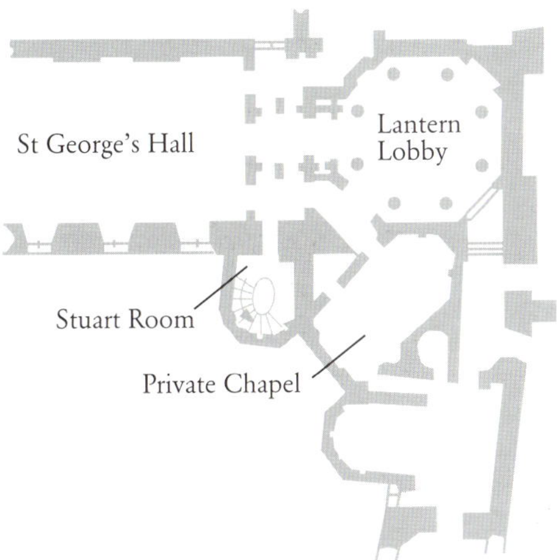

*The location of the new Private Chapel.*

# THE GREEN DRAWING ROOM

The serenity of the Green Drawing Room was a particular joy to paint. I had been daunted by the task ahead of me in the restored castle, by the richness and grandeur of the rooms, but I was reassured in the Green Drawing Room – which I had not painted after the fire. There a detail caught my eye one day: a cushion tassel was hanging over the edge of a sofa, silhouetted against the window. This became the key to the massive subjects in front of me, my starting point, and I drew it with abundant happiness! From then I drew voraciously; every chair, table, torchère and bronze was to be cherished, its great beauty to be caressed. By looking and drawing one becomes familiar with every object; the eye and the pencil travel around each exquisite shape, feeling the form and line. As I worked, the morning sunlight streaked across the carpet, lightening the ceiling and causing the colour of the silk damask to sing with life.

OPPOSITE: Although badly damaged by smoke and water, the Green Drawing Room largely survived the fire, which was stopped near the door into the adjacent Crimson Drawing Room.

The silk for the walls was replaced and the window curtains renewed to match more closely the designs made by Morel and Seddon for George IV in the 1820s. The seat furniture is part of a large set also commissioned by George IV from Morel and Seddon. The Axminster carpet, designed for Queen Victoria, was shown at the Great Exhibition in 1851. The display cases contain some of George IV's outstanding collection of Sèvres porcelain.

RL 33492
560 × 760 mm/22 × 30 in.
1998

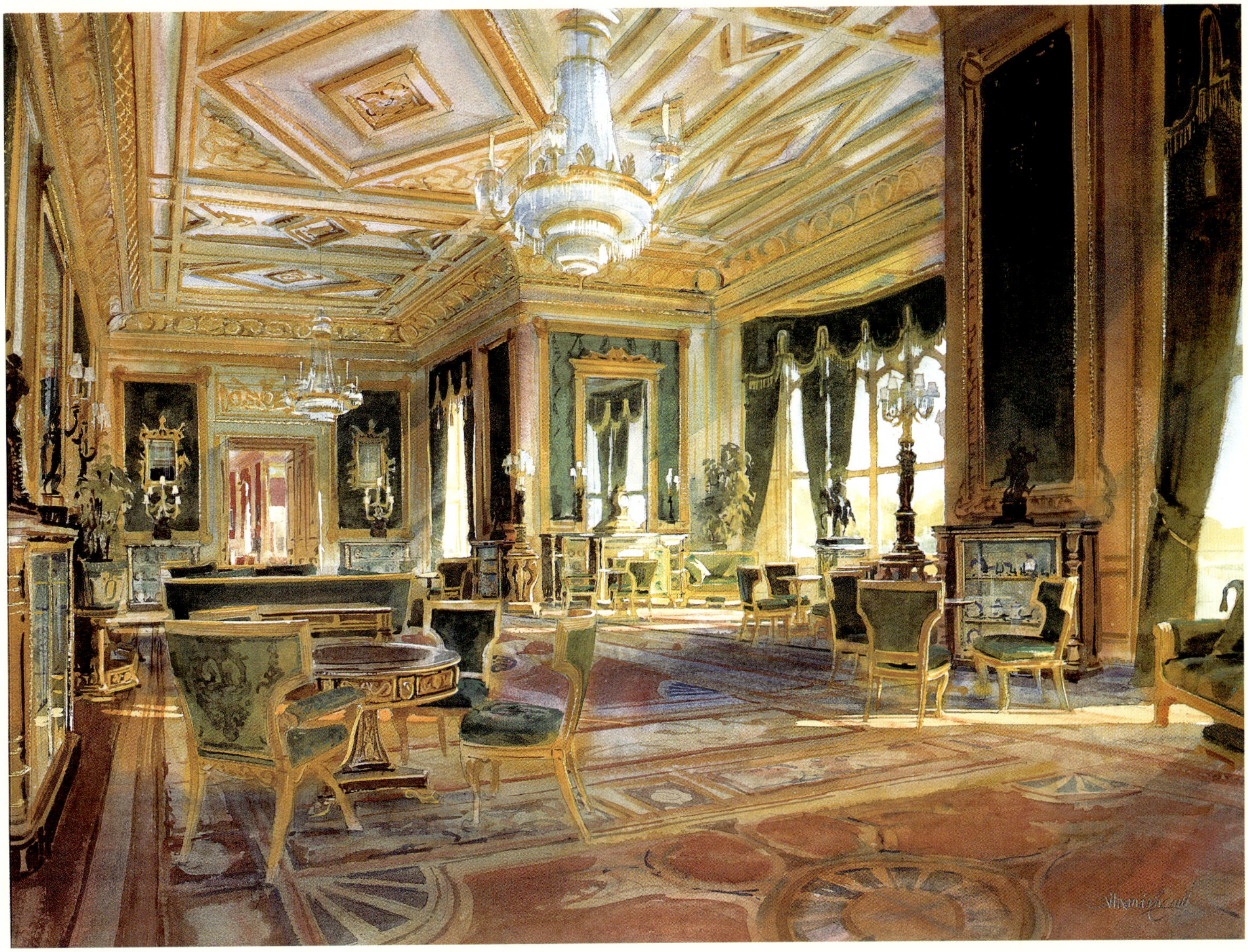

# THE CRIMSON DRAWING ROOM

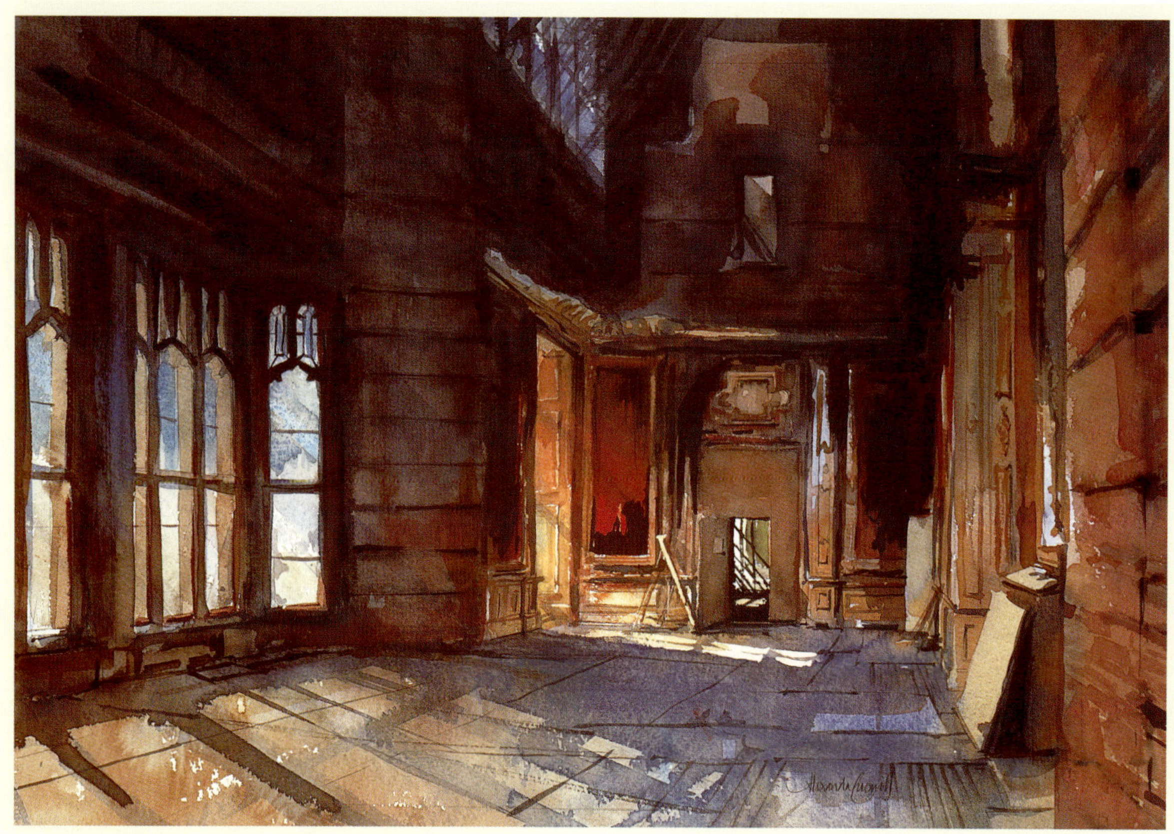

LEFT: The Crimson Drawing Room was totally destroyed during the fire, but its contents survived as they had been moved out during electrical rewiring work. Fortunately, fire-fighters prevented the fire from going far into the adjacent Green Drawing Room. Both rooms had been entirely remodelled by George IV's architect Sir Jeffry Wyatville in the 1820s as part of his major works on the east side of the castle.

RL 32538
380 × 560 mm/15 × 22 in.
1993

OPPOSITE: The Crimson Drawing Room was restored by Donald Insall and Partners. The reinstated ceiling incorporates many fragments of the original plasterwork by Francis Bernasconi. The large glass chandelier was severely damaged in the fire but has been completely restored. The new crimson silk for the curtains and walls is of the pattern originally used by Morel and Seddon in the 1820s.

RL 33493
560 × 760 mm/22 × 30 in.
1998

After the fire the Crimson Drawing Room had only scraps of damask left on its walls and its ceiling had disappeared, together with the rooms above. Underfoot the parquetry floor heaved and sagged where water had swollen the wood out of true. To one side of the door to the Green Drawing Room – partially blocked after the fire – I placed a step-ladder to give a sense of scale. A meagre morning sun percolates through the opaque windows, showing the ruined floor.

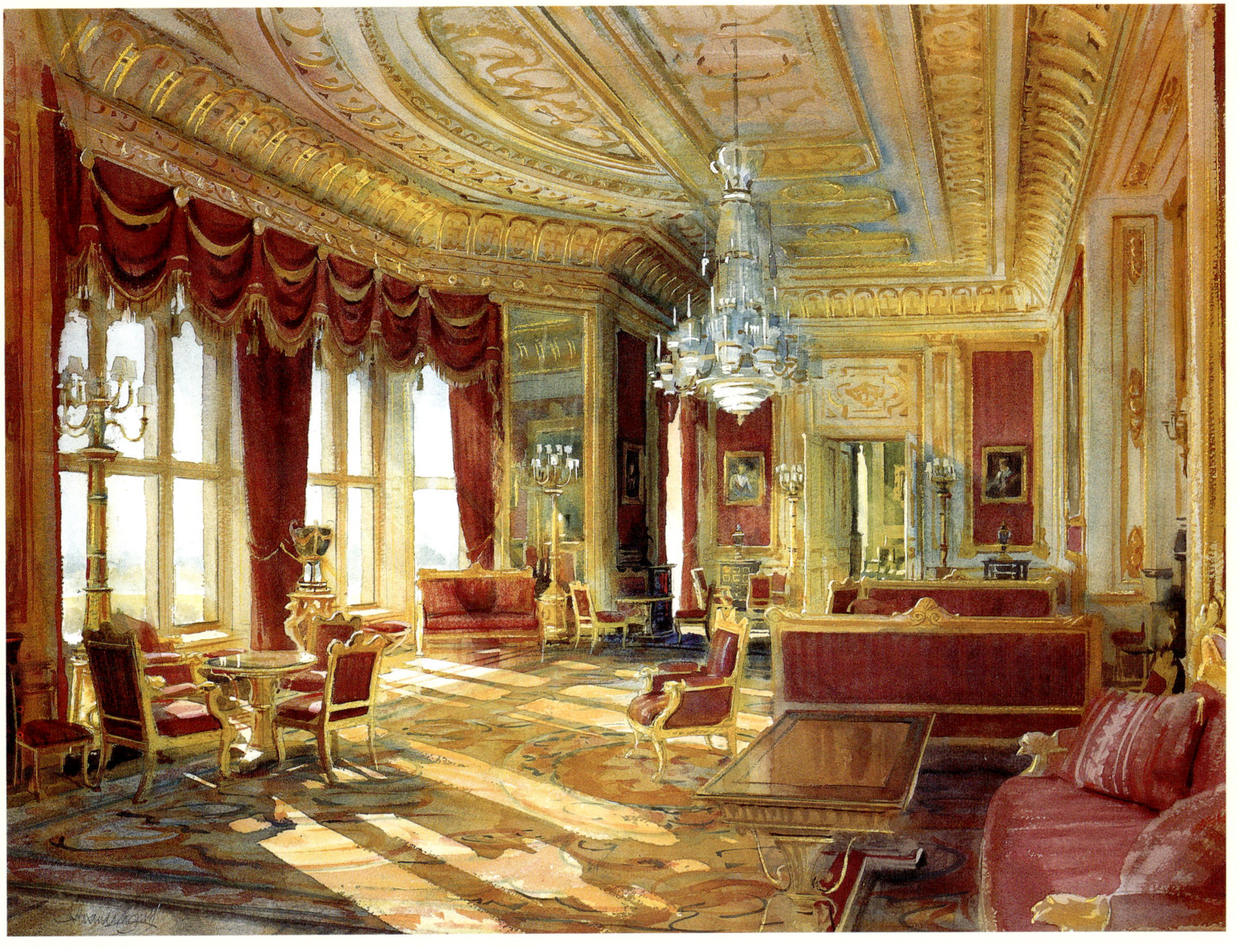

Since the restoration the morning sun has quite a startling effect; bright new crimson now infuses the room with a rosy glow, the new gilt shining like fragments of pure sunlight, and the whole room sounds a fanfare of optimism. I had been very careful about the light for these interiors. The joys of surface, texture and plane, with the magic of air, atmosphere and volume, can best be demonstrated by the interplay of light and shade. Reflected light lifts the heaviest burden, its weight graced with a lyrical quality that can lift it out of reality and into the sublime.

# THE STATE DINING ROOM

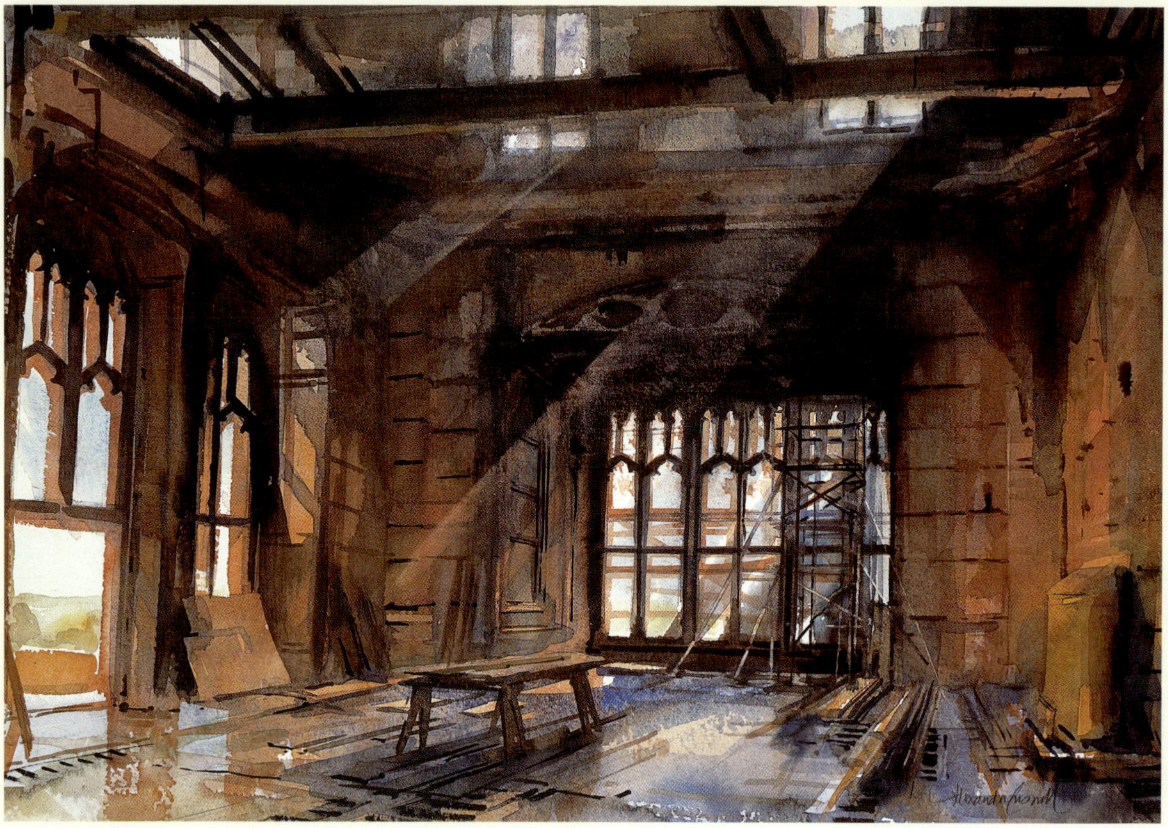

The State Dining Room and the rooms in the Prince of Wales's Tower above it were totally destroyed during the fire. Apart from one large painting and one large sideboard the entire contents of the State Dining Room were saved as they had been removed during electrical rewiring work. The cast-iron ceiling girders also survived; they date from 1853, when a previous firc damaged the room.

RL 32540
380 × 560 mm/15 × 22 in.
1993

In the State Dining Room, the destruction was just as comprehensive as in the adjacent Crimson Drawing Room; by the time the rubble had been cleared almost nothing remained of the room but charred purple brickwork and twisted iron girders. The floor was largely intact but carbonised and the carved panelling around the windows was the same – a perfect representation of its former self in charcoal. A tower of scaffolding in the window bay drew a confused filigree of lines against the light, and in the middle of the floor a trestle table provided a bad pun on the room's former glory.

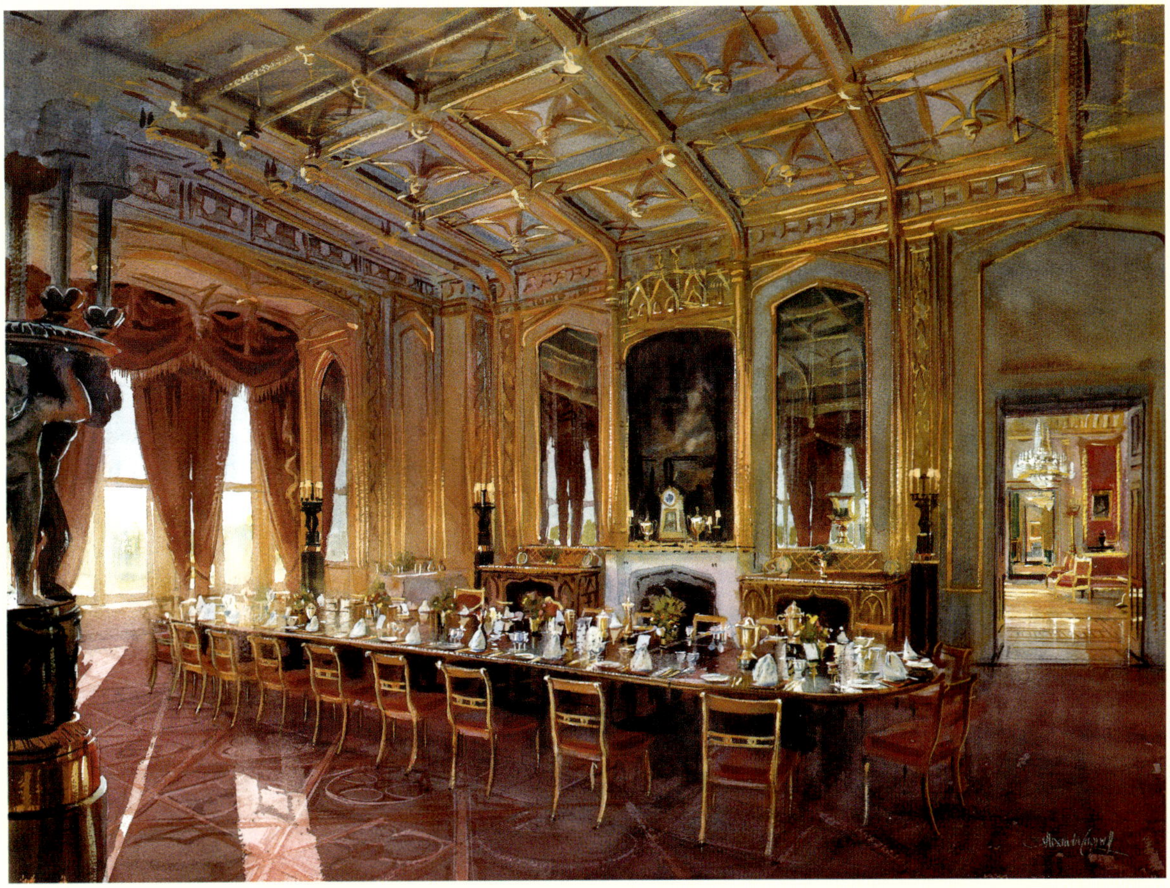

The State Dining Room has been restored in the Gothic style, as it was originally designed for George IV by his architect Sir Jeffry Wyatville in the 1820s. The new crimson curtains and carpet reflect the original Morel and Seddon scheme for George IV; the sideboards were also supplied in the late 1820s. The bronze lamps were made in 1810 for Carlton House, George IV's London residence.

The table is laid for guests at one of the lunches given by The Queen each year in June, during the Royal Ascot race meeting.

RL 33494
560 × 760 mm/22 × 30 in.
1998

After the restoration the glory came flooding back, the table laid with gold and crystal once again. I had chosen a new viewpoint for this painting, allowing me to show off the wonderful enfilade through the Crimson and Green Drawing Rooms to the White Drawing Room beyond, all radiant in the morning sun. The sequence of rooms was like a résumé of all the goodness that the restoration had achieved. From that position with careful fidgeting I could also capture the reflection in the mirror of the fabulous Russian vase that stands in the north window, otherwise hidden by the chubby cherubs of the Vulliamy bronze torchère on the left-hand edge of the painting.

# THE OCTAGON DINING ROOM

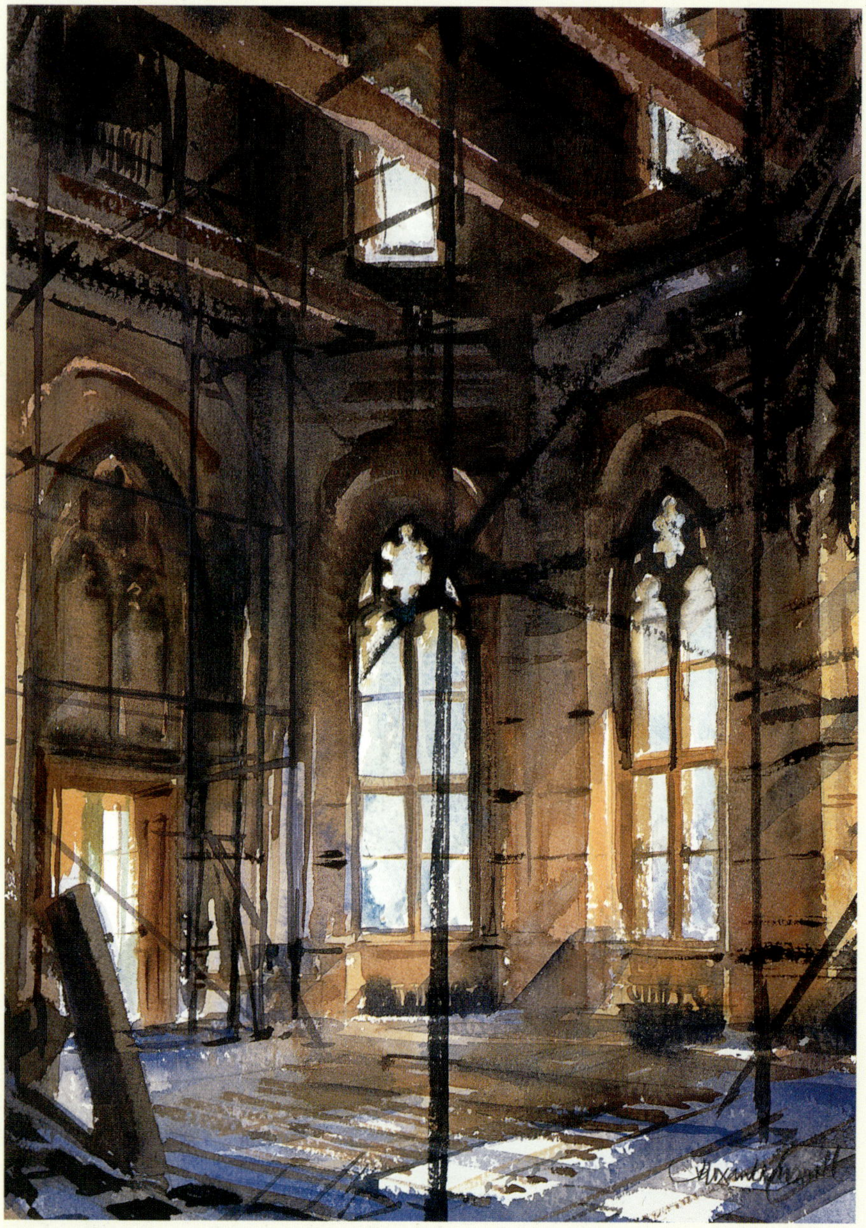

Turning round from the viewpoint of the restored State Dining Room, the Octagon Dining Room is revealed. It had been totally destroyed by the fire, and by the time I painted it just a framework of scaffolding lined the tower.

Five years later rich red curtains (opposite) frame the windows once more, and the furniture and chandelier designed by the young Augustus Pugin are bathed in sunshine. A mirror on the left-hand edge of the painting allowed me to show part of another window. Behind that mirror a secret door leads through the China Corridor to the Grand Reception Room.

RIGHT: The Octagon Dining Room has been restored in the Gothic style favoured by George IV and his architect Sir Jeffry Wyatville in the 1820s. The gilt metal Gothic chandelier was made for this room in 1828; badly damaged in the fire, it has now been completely restored.

RL 33499
560 × 380 mm/22 × 15 in.
1998

OPPOSITE: It was in the Octagon Dining Room that the fire finally burnt itself out during the night of 20 November 1992. The room is on the principal floor of the Brunswick Tower, built by George IV in the late 1820s. It is at the north-east corner of the castle. Fire-fighters encouraged the fire into this corner as it could go no further. The three floors above were consumed in a dramatic tower of fire which could be seen for miles around.

RL 32544
380 × 280 mm/15 × 11 in.
1993

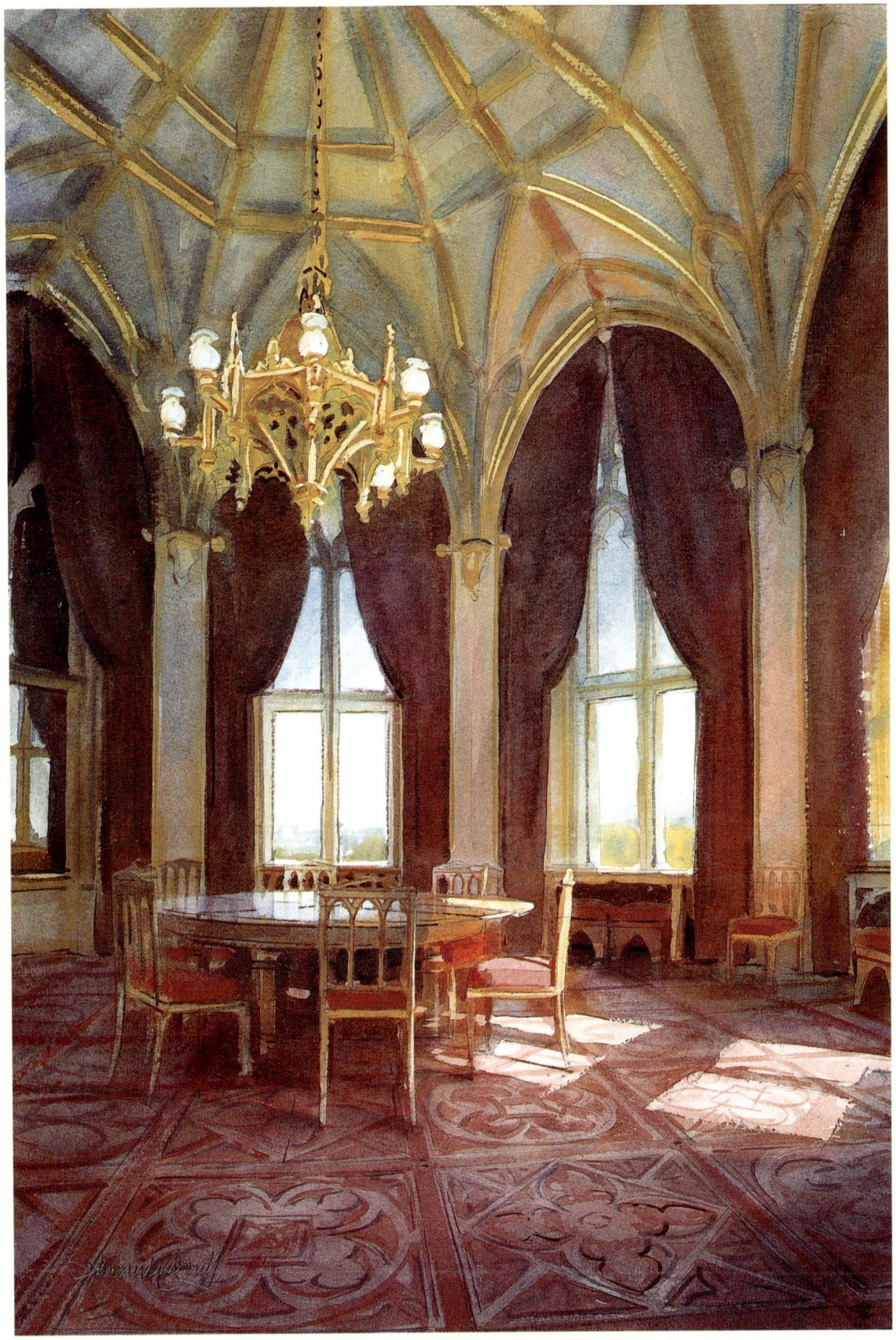

# THE GRAND RECEPTION ROOM

The image of the Grand Reception Room after the fire, with its malachite vase standing defiant and complete in front of the window, is a potent one; the fire had spread from the Private Chapel through St George's Hall and into the roof of the Grand Reception Room. When I saw it for the first time, sunlight filtered through the fretwork of beams, illuminating mud-streaked gilt plasterwork and shattered mirrors. The contrast between order and chaos was acute. The interior had become an exterior – exposed, naked. The room was not as badly damaged as some and its recognisable interior is incongruous, never having been seen before with sunlight from above. In my painting I placed a workman with a ladder next to the malachite vase to persuade the viewer of the sheer size of the vase, and reveal the scale of the whole room.

OPPOSITE: The Grand Reception Room was created by George IV in the late 1820s from Charles II's Guard Chamber. It is one of the earliest examples of the rococo revival in Britain.

The room's elaborate plaster ceiling was destroyed in the fire, but the wall panelling remained largely unscathed. The furniture and the six large eighteenth-century Gobelins tapestries which hung on the walls were removed before the fire reached the room. The large Russian malachite vase at the north end of the room, which remained in situ, was only slightly damaged.

RL 32539
380 × 560 mm/15 × 22 in.
1993

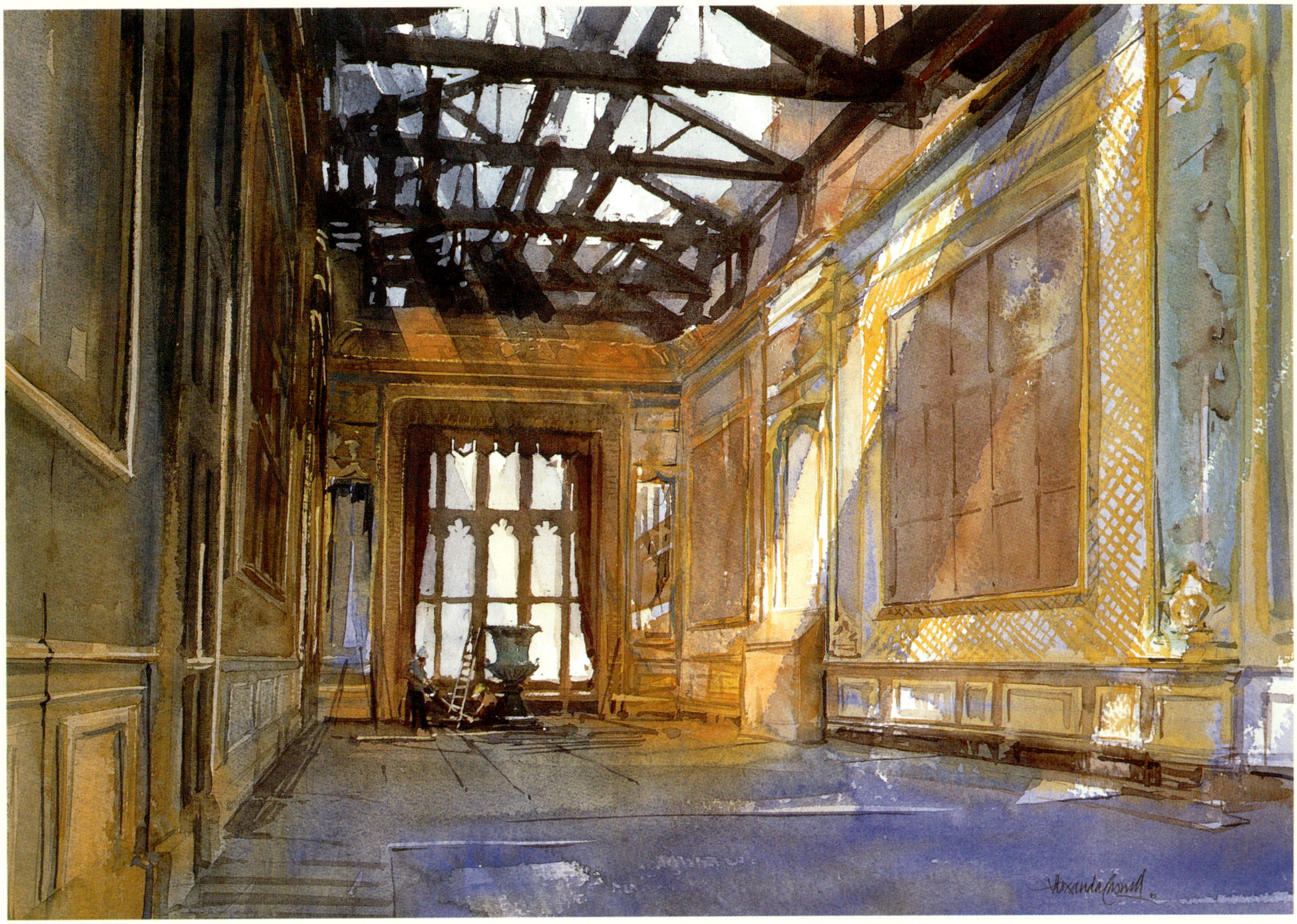

Painted from exactly the same viewpoint after the restoration, the room gave its own scale with the furniture back in the room and the rugs floating on the shiny floor. The malachite vase presides over all like a veteran survivor enthroned below the new *passementerie* of the curtains. New mirrors between the tapestries reflect part of the window, multiplying the light in the room.

Here, perhaps more than in any other room, the contrast between the fire damage and the restored room is at its most subtle since the visual comparison is not so striking as elsewhere. The view of this room in its restored splendour could easily have been painted the day before the fire broke out; suddenly the continuum of time is in doubt and the definitions of which is 'before' and which 'after' become more confusing. Other rooms had been redesigned and built as new spaces – they had never been seen before, never painted before.

The life of Windsor Castle will continue beyond our own, and I am privileged to imagine that my watercolours of the effects of disaster and rebirth may help to tell the tale of those years in the last decade of the twentieth century.

OPPOSITE: The Grand Reception Room has been restored to its original form. The ceiling, first modelled by Francis Bernasconi, has been reconstructed and the magnificent gilding renewed; the six Gobelins tapestries have been put back and the three gilt bronze and glass chandeliers repaired and rehung. The parquetry floor is the restored original.

RL 33495
560 × 760 mm/22 × 30 in.
1998

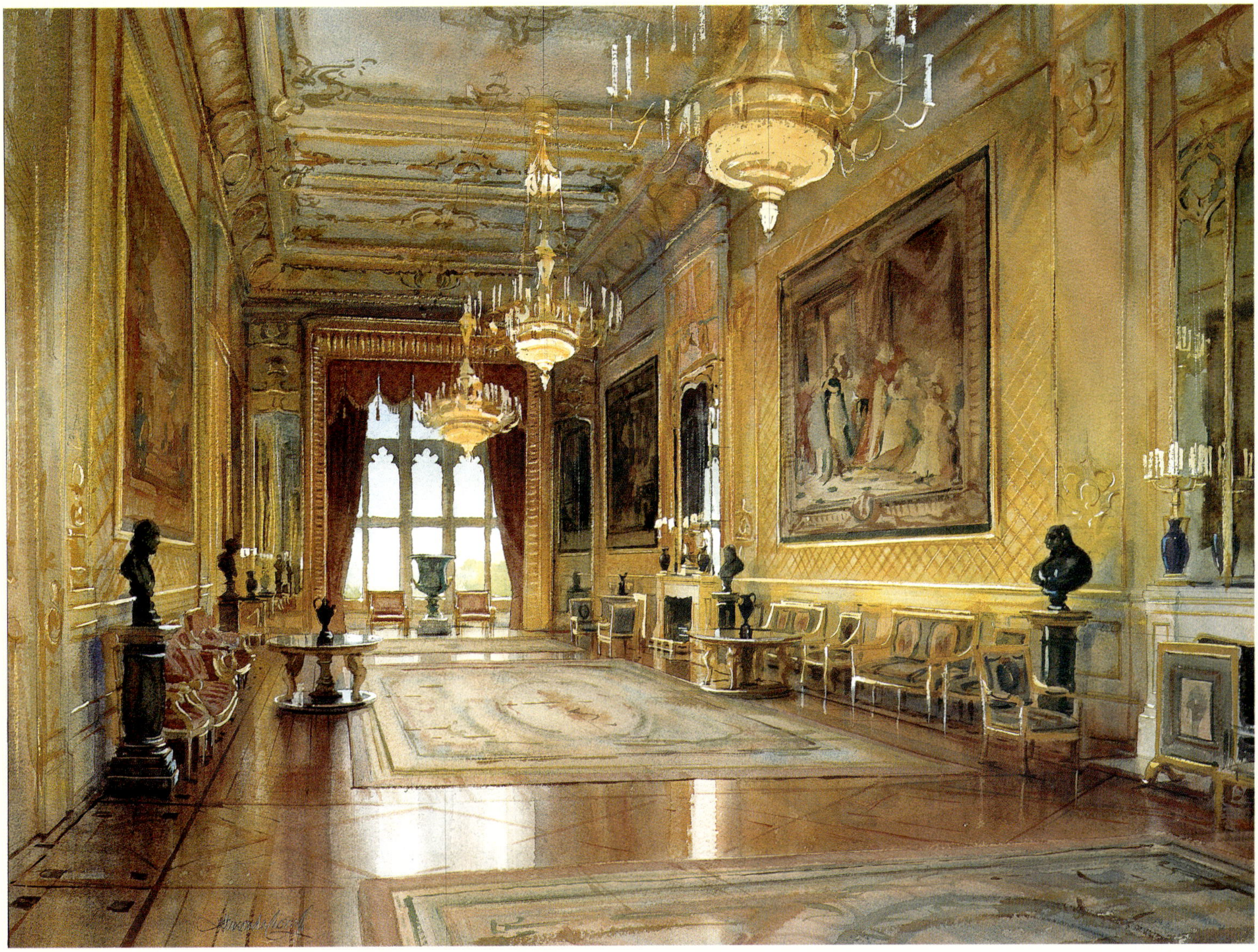

## PLAN OF THE FIRE-DAMAGED AREA OF WINDSOR CASTLE

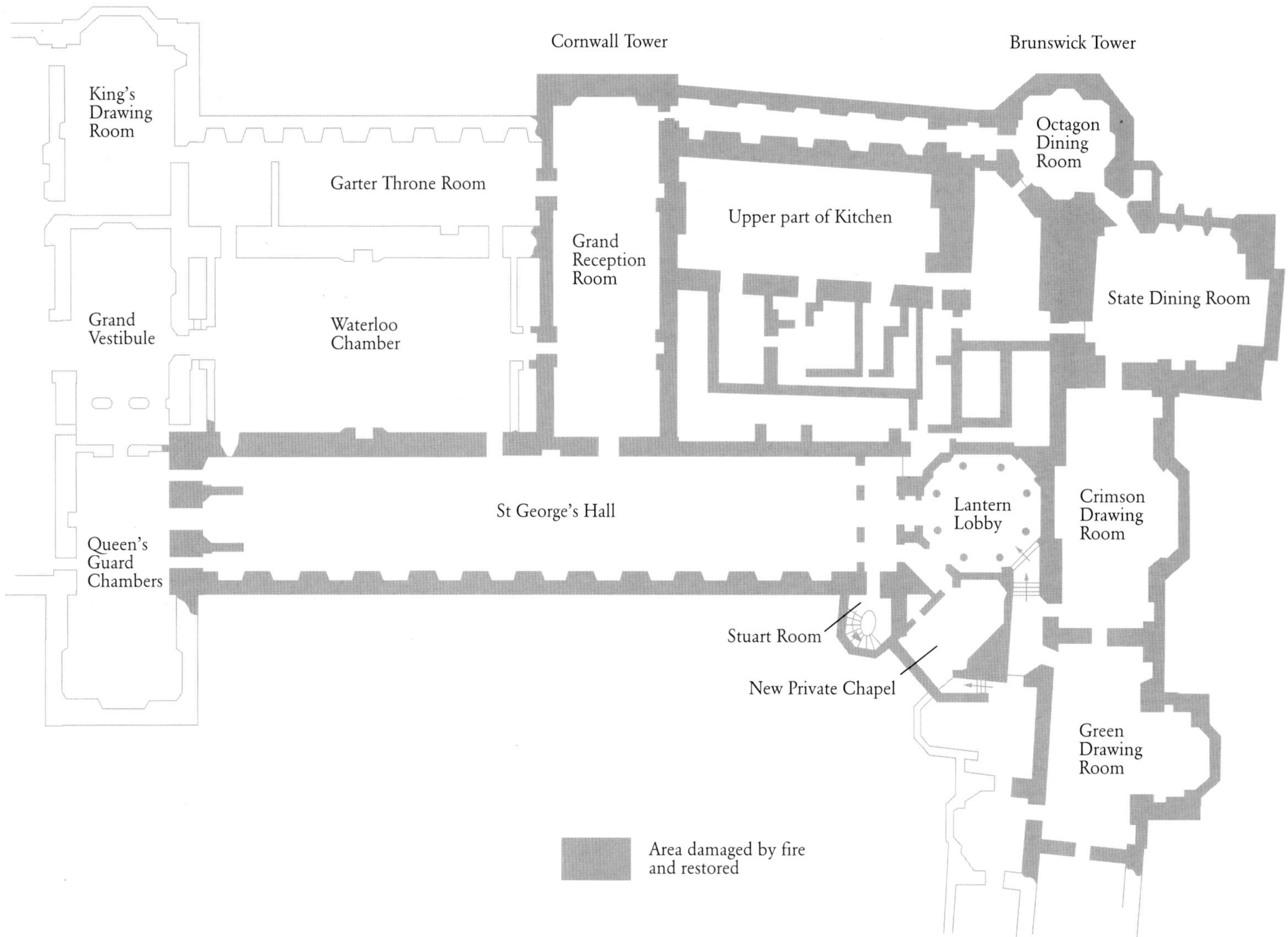


## FURTHER READING

Steven Brindle and Brian Kerr, *Windsor Revealed. New Light on the History of the Castle*, London 1997
Adam Nicolson, *Restoration. The Rebuilding of Windsor Castle*, London 1997
John Martin Robinson, *Royal Palaces. Windsor Castle. A Short History*. London 1996
John Martin Robinson, *Windsor Castle* (official guide), London 1998